EFFECTIVE
SURVIVAL STRATEGIES™

Defeating
DEPRESSION

Y. S. LIN

ROSEN
PUBLISHING®

New York

Published in 2016 by The Rosen Publishing Group, Inc.
29 East 21st Street, New York, NY 10010

Library of Congress Cataloging-in-Publication Data

Lin, Y. S.
Defeating depression / Y. S. Lin. — First edition.
    pages cm. — (Effective survival strategies)
Audience: Grades 7–12.
Includes bibliographical references and index.
ISBN 978-1-4994-6175-6 (library bound)
1. Depression in children—Juvenile literature. I. Title.
RJ506.D4L56 2016
618.92'8527—dc23
                    2015025085

For many of the images in this book, the people photographed are models. The depictions do not imply actual situations or events.

Manufactured in China

Contents

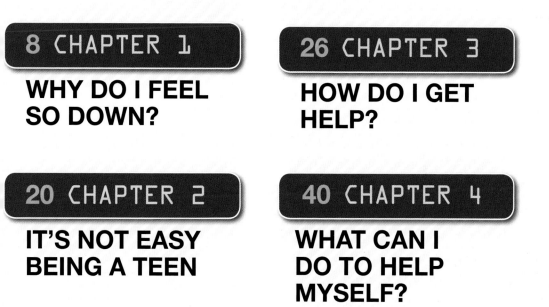

Introduction

Being a teen is very demanding. Keeping up with homework, going through puberty, and dealing with unfamiliar emotions is challenging enough. But many teens today also work part-time, babysit younger siblings, help with chores, resist peer pressure, deal with cyberbullying, participate in extracurricular activities, and find time to hang out with family and friends. That is a lot to juggle! It is no wonder that teens occasionally feel tired, stressed out, or even a bit down. These are normal feelings that all people face from time to time.

It is when you start to feel sad or more tired than usual for weeks on end, no longer enjoy favorite activities, or begin to have feelings of worthlessness or hopelessness that you need to pay more attention to what is going on. These are all possible warning signs of a serious medical condition called depression. It is important to know that when someone suffers from depression, it does not mean that the person is crazy. It also does not mean the person is weak, lazy, or bad. Many successful people have suffered from depression at some point in their lives. Demi Lovato, Brad Pitt, J. K. Rowling, Charles Darwin, and Abraham Lincoln are just a few famous people who have accomplished impressive things despite having battled depression.

Many teens experience high levels of stress. A survey by the American Psychological Association found that the top sources of stress for teens are school and deciding what to do after graduation.

What having depression does mean is that a person needs help, just as one would go to the doctor when suffering from migraines or chronic stomach pains. If you are diagnosed with depression by a health professional, there is help out there and you can get better. Keep in mind that if you suffer from depression, you are not alone. According to the National Institutes of Mental Health (NIMH) website, more than one in ten adolescents suffer from a depressive disorder before they reach the age of eighteen. Some experts believe the number is higher. Depression has been shown to affect girls and boys of all different ages and backgrounds. Anyone can suffer from depression, even people who you think are attractive, popular, and smart.

Depression is something human beings have been aware of for thousands of years. Hippocrates, a great physician in ancient Greece, described what we call depression today as an illness. For thousands of years, views on depression ranged from the incomplete to the ignorant. Many different treatments were concocted. Sadly, for those suffering from depression in the past there was little hope of getting better.

Fortunately, depression is better understood today. There are trained professionals who help teens suffering from depression. There are also medications that can dramatically lessen the symptoms. Furthermore, there continue to be advances in science revealing more about what causes depression and hinting at promising new treatments on the horizon. Additionally, in the

Depression is a serious problem. You can get better if you suffer from depression, but you need expert help. Trying to tough it out, ignoring the problem, or self-medicating is dangerous and can make things much worse.

United States, there now exists a law called the Mental Health Parity and Addiction Equity Act. This means that health insurance companies and government health programs must treat mental health issues as they would any other illness, like diabetes or arthritis. This legislation makes treatments for depression accessible to more people.

If you think you might be suffering from depression:

- DON'T hide it.
- DON'T try to tough it out.
- DON'T ignore it and hope that it will go away on its own.

Depression is a serious problem, and you need help to get better. This resource will help you get an understanding of what depression is, which symptoms are most common among teens, which online and offline resources are best for you and your family, and most important, how you can get help today and start on a confident path to feeling better and stronger.

CHAPTER 1

WHY DO I FEEL SO DOWN?

"**I** am so depressed." It is a phrase that is often casually used to describe feeling temporarily disappointed, frustrated, or unhappy. Most of us have uttered these words countless times. But saying you are "depressed" about something is vastly different from having a depressive disorder. Having a depressive disorder, or what people often generally call depression, is not a fleeting mood. It's a painful illness that needs to be treated.

Kinds of Depressive Disorders

There are many depressive disorders. Some, like seasonal affective disorder and postpartum depression, affect people during certain times of the year or at specific phases of their lives. Major depression is the most common form of depression. Others include persistent depressive disorder and bipolar disorder, which though less common is a serious form of mental illness that can be difficult to diagnose in teens.

Depression is a common, but complex, problem that comes in different forms. If you look at the ADAA website, there are eight different types of depression listed. The most common one is major depression.

Major depression is by far the most common of the depressive disorders. Unless indicated, most of the times when we mention "depression" in this resource we are referring to this illness. According to the NIMH website, about 7 percent of the adult population suffers from it at any given time. According to the same source, in 2012 about 9 percent of people between the ages of twelve and seventeen suffered from major depression. This means that if you walked into a classroom of thirty of your classmates, chances are that around three people would be struggling with symptoms of major depression at that time. The Anxiety Disorders Association of America (ADAA) website states that almost one in five Americans will suffer from major depression at some point in his or her life.

Depression is a serious problem that affects a large number of people. It is important to remind yourself of this because oftentimes teens suffer alone in silence, not realizing that people around them might be facing similar problems. By talking about it with people you trust, you may find more understanding than you expected and you very well could help someone else through a difficult time.

It's normal to be down if you get a bad grade or to feel sad if you get in an argument with a close friend. But when these negative feelings last for weeks or months, then it might be depression.

The teenage years are full of transitions and challenges, and it is normal for teens to have good and bad days. For instance, if you get into an argument with your best friend, get a bad grade on a math test, or break up with your first boyfriend or girlfriend, you might feel disappointed or sad for a while. In fact, it would be unusual if these kinds of events did not affect you. It is when these negative feelings last for weeks or even months and cause you to be unable to complete important tasks or enjoy even your favorite activities that you may have a more serious problem.

The Signs of Depression

There are many signs and symptoms of depression. Because each person is unique, he or she will experience depression differently than the next person. Still, there are some common elements. Answering "yes" to some of the following questions might indicate that you have symptoms of major depression:

- Have you felt a change in mood lately?
- Do you feel sadder, more anxious, or less excited than usual?
- Do you feel unusually irritable?
- Do you feel guilty or have feelings of worthlessness?
- Do you feel that your sleep habits and appetite have changed?
- Are you suddenly gaining weight or losing weight?
- Do you feel more tired than usual or less motivated in school?
- Are you having trouble concentrating in class or making decisions?
- Are you using alcohol, cigarettes, or drugs to try to make yourself feel better?
- Are you having headaches or stomachaches?
- Do you feel that you are thinking or moving slower than usual?

There are health issues that can mimic the symptoms of depression. A lack of certain nutrients or thyroid problems could cause mood regulation problems. Only a medical professional can make an accurate diagnosis.

- Do you find it difficult to enjoy yourself?
- Have you had thoughts of hurting yourself or taking your own life?

Only a doctor or mental health professional can diagnose you with depression. It is too hard to diagnose yourself by checking off a list, and it is very difficult for most people to judge their own behavior accurately. Teens also sometimes exhibit unique signs of depression, like getting in trouble at school, skipping classes, or feeling misunderstood. Also, there are other health conditions that might cause you to have some of the symptoms above, and a health care professional can help you sort these things out.

Persistent depressive disorder is a chronic form of depression that generally causes milder symptoms than major depression

Depression often looks different in teens than in adults. For example, teens that teachers or parents might label as "lazy" because they are sleeping a lot or are unable to focus in class might very well have depression.

but lasts at least two years. A teen suffering from persistent depressive disorder often has it awhile before anyone notices. For instance, parents and friends might think the person is just moody, pessimistic, or negative because the individual symptoms are often not as obvious as in major depression. Still, persistent depressive disorder can last for years and impact a person's quality of life, self-esteem, and relationships with others.

Another depressive disorder is called bipolar disorder. Teens suffering from bipolar disorder experience episodes of major depression and then periods of mania—feeling unusually energetic, creative, or powerful. During manic periods, a person will often behave unpredictably. Manic episodes can be dangerous because during these times the person is likely to engage in risky behavior due to a distorted sense of his or her own abilities and the inability to make good decisions.

Depressive disorders rarely go away on their own as the cold or flu might. People suffering from any of these disorders need professional help to stop them from getting worse. With help there is a very good chance of getting better. Some people might

SUICIDAL THOUGHTS: GET HELP NOW!

If you ever have any thoughts of harming yourself or taking your own life, you need to reach out for help NOW. What you are feeling is temporary, and no matter how bad you feel right at this moment you can get better and enjoy life again. Please tell a parent, a teacher, or another trusted adult immediately. If this is not possible, you can call the National Suicide Prevention Line at: 1-800-273-8255. In an emergency please call 911.

suffer only one episode of major depression in their lives, but more often, a person might experience several periods of depression throughout his or her lifetime. This does not mean it is hopeless. These episodes of depression can be treated. You are not alone. There are many resources out there and many professionals in your community who have the expertise to help you get better.

A Look at the Brain

Like all diseases, there is a biological basis to depression. This means that there are chemical and physical changes going on inside your brain that are causing the symptoms of depression. The brain is the most complex and mysterious organ in the human body. In the past few decades, though, neuroscientists have learned a lot more about the brain. This has helped us better understand depression.

The brain is made up of a hundred billion neurons, specialized cells that can communicate with each other using traveling electrical signals and special chemicals called neurotransmitters. The neurotransmitters, acting like chemical messages, travel over a tiny gap between neurons, called a synapse, either exciting or inhibiting a response. Some people compare the network of neurons to an electrical circuit board. One important neurotransmitter that plays a big role in regulating mood is serotonin. If cells secrete too little serotonin, have malfunctioning receptors (parts that receive the chemical messages), or have too little serotonin present in the synapses, one possible result is depression. Serotonin might also explain why exercise helps with mood. When a person works out, the levels of serotonin in his or her blood increase. As a result, the person might feel happier and more energetic. The exact mechanism of how this works

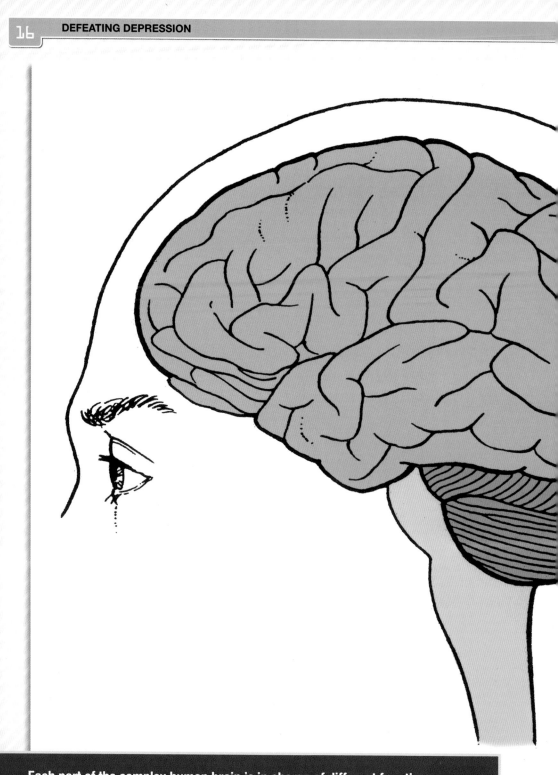

Each part of the complex human brain is in charge of different functions. The cerebrum (*blue*) allows us to form memories, regulate emotions, and learn languages. The cerebellum (*green*) coordinates movements.

is still unclear. Scientists believe that depression results when the levels of several neurotransmitters are not regulated properly.

The brain is made up of many parts, and each part has its own important and unique function. For example, the cerebellum is in charge of coordinating movement. The cerebrum controls emotions and allows us to form memories. Scientists are able to use a special technique called magnetic resonance imaging (MRI) to look at the different parts of the brain and study the activity going on in each area. They have found that in many people suffering from depression, the hippocampus, an area of the cerebrum that helps people form memories, looks smaller than people who are healthy.

Understanding what goes on in the brain helps us better understand why people suffer from depression. It reminds us that when someone suffers from depression, it is not his or her fault. It is a medical problem, and it is treatable.

Why Is It Happening to Me?

Teens suffering from depression often wonder, "Why is this happening to me?" The truth is that depression is complicated and usually there are many factors at play. For example, the fact that depression tends to affect more females than males implies that the fluctuations in hormones in females after puberty can contribute to it.

Even today's best scientists know that they do not yet fully grasp all the causes of depression. However, we do have an idea of some of the contributing factors.

It's in the Genes

Genes, which people inherit from both of their parents, play a big role in depression. Our genes spell out instructions to make proteins that allow our bodies to function. People who inherit faulty genes from their parents are more likely to become depressed. For example, scientists believe that the gene 5-HTT partly determines how susceptible someone is to depression when faced with stress.

If someone in your immediate family suffers from major depression, you are at an increased risk for depression. According to the Harvard Medical School website, if one identical twin suffers from bipolar disorder, there is an 80 percent chance that the other twin will as well.

It's the Environment

We must also consider environmental factors that can trigger episodes of depression. In fact, scientists believe that the environment is as important or more important than genetic predisposition. Some factors that have been shown to be triggers are poverty, parental neglect, trauma and loss, childhood abuse, bullying, a lack of sunlight, excessive social media or Internet use, and certain chronic health issues. The lack of a support system, being part of a marginalized community, and having anxiety disorders, learning disabilities, attention deficit disorder, or other psychological issues can also be contributing factors.

It's a Little Bit Random

It should be noted that usually a combination of several factors lead someone to suffer from depression. For example, just because a parent has depression doesn't necessarily mean that you will. Some people face many of the obstacles that are listed here but do not suffer from depression. Then there are some people who have depression without obvious risk factors.

CHAPTER 2

IT'S NOT EASY BEING A TEEN

Being a teenager is by no means an easy job. The adolescent years have always been a challenge due to hormones that are in flux; the complicated, but necessary, struggle to become more independent from one's parents; and the changing nature of relationships around you, both platonic and romantic. Today's teens have more access to technology, information, travel, and culture than any other generation before them. But they also face many new challenges, and it is no wonder that teen depression, along with other mental health issues, has been on the rise.

Technology

There has never been a time where it was so easy to communicate with people near and far. With Facebook, Twitter, Instagram, text messaging, video chatting, and smartphones, technology

According to a Pew Research Study, 71 percent of teens use more than one social media site. Social media is one way for teens to connect with friends and family near and far, but too much of it can actually be isolating.

allows teens to easily keep tabs on what their friends are doing after school, share pictures and videos on their social networks, and keep in touch with family near and far.

Still, there are dangers associated with these technologies, some more obvious than others. Studies have shown that people are less likely to connect in person now that it is easier to just text or post a Facebook message. Less face-to-face time can lead to feelings of isolation. This might seem counterintuitive because you might wonder how you can be lonely when you have hundreds of Facebook friends. Well, when people interact online, they do not experience the same connection as they would when sharing a meal with someone, for instance. Furthermore, people present only a certain aspect of themselves on social media. When someone chooses to put something online, usually the post is something that will put him or her in a flattering light. Most people want to appear fun or popular and may choose not to share anything that speaks to challenges they are facing. As a result, many teens falsely believe that everyone else around them is happier than they are.

Drugs, Alcohol, and Other Addictions

Sometimes, people who are feeling bad turn to alcohol and drugs to numb their pain or get a temporary high. However these "feel good" effects are short-lived, and then more of the substance is needed the next time to get the same effect. Also, many of these substances ultimately make you feel worse and leave you scrambling to find other ways to feel better. Drugs, alcohol, and cigarettes all have dangerous side effects, particularly in young people. Adolescents are more likely to get addicted and experience negative changes in the brain and are more susceptible to other kinds of health problems.

Some newer risks teens face today are "designer drugs" that can be bought online and misunderstandings regarding the safety of marijuana. Teens should never use these so-called designer drugs. They can be extremely dangerous and even deadly as they are neither regulated nor safe. As for marijuana, there is a notion that it is safe, especially after the legalization of marijuana for adults in some states. Marijuana may be relatively safe for mature brains (though this is still being debated), but it is not safe for young people. The drug causes changes in developing brains and can have long-term effects on learning, thinking, and memory. Studies have shown that regular marijuana use by teens can lower their IQs permanently, impair judgment, and lead to poor decisions and accidents.

Obesity, Processed Food, and Lack of Exercise

According to the Centers for Disease Control and Prevention (CDC), the percentage of adolescents aged twelve to nineteen who suffered from obesity went from 5 percent to nearly 21 percent between 1980 and 2012. Part of this epidemic is due to eating more processed, high caloric foods and getting less exercise. Studies have found that obesity and depression are closely linked. Those who are obese are more likely to be depressed because of low self-esteem, feelings of isolation, and less mobility. Those who are depressed are less likely to eat healthily and lose weight when they need to.

WORKING WITH ADOLESCENT PATIENTS

Dr. Maria Master, an attending psychiatrist and neuroethicist at New York Presbyterian Hospital–Cornell Medical College who also has a private practice, explained, "Adolescents often have creative minds and fresh ways of seeing the world—it is interesting to be a part of someone's life just as they are learning about the power of their mind and feelings. Adolescence is also often a stressful time, full of new challenges, conflicts and desires, so there are genuine and important issues to solve."

When asked about barriers to treatment, she said, "The biggest

(continued on the next page)

(continued from the previous page)

social barriers to treatment are cost and stigma, and we hope to see more people gain access to high quality care as society realizes just how life saving it can be. In explaining your decision to start therapy, it may help to remind others that therapy is designed to help you be the best person you can be. In this regard, top athletes and performers work with therapists to help them compete and perform at the highest levels. It's not that different from what you might do in therapy—understand and change anything blocking you from achieving your most important goals in life.

Parents and teachers should consider that sometimes depression looks different in young men versus women. For example, if an adolescent boy starts getting in more fights, using drugs or drinking heavily, or having a lot of 'accidents'—consider depression. If an adolescent girl becomes overly focused on weight or dieting, or starts injuring herself or has temperamental outbursts—consider depression. These are just a few symptoms that get labeled 'bad behavior' but actually may point to a psychiatric condition that could improve with compassionate treatment."

Fierce Competition

In this fast-paced world, teens feel more pressure than ever. Many students feel that to compete in the future they need to do well in school, participate in many activities, and get into the best college possible. We hear on the news all the time that college admission rates are going down and more and more qualified students are being rejected from the college of their dreams. There are many pressures associated with doing well in school and getting into college, while maintaining an active

Being a teen today is challenging. More and more students have to juggle homework, multiple extracurricular activities, social media, and time with friends and family. The pressure to succeed is often intense.

social life, including on social media. These pressures can leave teens feeling overwhelmed.

Multicultural Environment

The United States is a more diverse place than ever. Much of the world is experiencing a similar rise in multiculturalism. Increasing diversity enriches communities and broadens our horizons. Still, it must be acknowledged that there are challenges that come along with this increase in diversity. Many minorities and new immigrants experience racism, limited opportunities, police profiling, and stereotyping. These are all huge stressors that can contribute to a higher rate of depression.

CHAPTER 3

HOW DO I GET HELP?

Once you decide that you need help, you may wonder where you should start. The good news is that there are many options. The challenge is that it will most likely take some effort to find the best treatment for you. For some teens, talk therapy with a qualified professional will be enough. For many, medications and psychotherapy together make the most effective option. The great news is that with the right combination of medication and psychotherapy, success rates for treatments are high. According to the NIMH website, a study has shown that it is estimated that up to 85 percent of adolescents will respond to treatment after participating in therapy and taking antidepressants for thirty-six weeks.

You will probably find that you need some assistance finding help. It is useful to have a parent, grandparent, or other trusted adult help you make appointments and drive you to them. An adult can help you navigate the confusing waters of health

Talking to your parents is often the first step to getting help. If that is not an option, grandparents, coaches, or school counselors are just some examples of adults who would likely be willing to help you find the help you need.

insurance coverage and weigh the risks and benefits of certain medications. Another great reason for talking to a trusted adult is that when depressed, you may lose motivation and find it difficult to make decisions. It is a cruel fact of depression that the illness itself will make it much harder for you to get the help you need. A trusted adult can provide encouragement when you need it.

Talk to the Experts

The best place to start is a visit to your pediatrician or family doctor. At the office, the doctor will ask you questions about your medical history and talk to you about how you have been feeling physically and mentally. Through these questions, he or she will get a better sense of what is going on. The doctor will likely do a physical exam and some blood tests to rule out other medical conditions that could be causing your symptoms. For example, problems with your thyroid could cause symptoms like those of depression. A lack of vitamin D, which can cause fatigue, sleep problems, and lack of energy, is often be confused with depression. If your doctor finds one of these problems, she will address it. If she believes that you are suffering from depression, she will recommend next steps, such as seeing a therapist.

Finding a Therapist

There are several types of therapists that you can meet with. The first is a psychiatrist, who has been trained as a medical doctor and specializes in treating mental health issues. A psychiatrist can prescribe medication, do talk therapy, and order medical tests. For more severe depression, a psychiatrist is usually necessary because medication is normally part of the treatment.

A clinical psychologist is a mental health professional who has an advanced degree called a doctorate in psychology. This means that the person has spent many years studying how to treat mental health issues. Clinical psychologists are trained to diagnose and treat anxiety, depression, and other mental health issues. They are often experts at certain types of therapies, including cognitive behavioral, biofeedback, or psychodynamic therapies.

A clinical social worker is a trained professional with a master's degree in social work. Clinical social workers often work with people who are facing life difficulties or mental health issues.

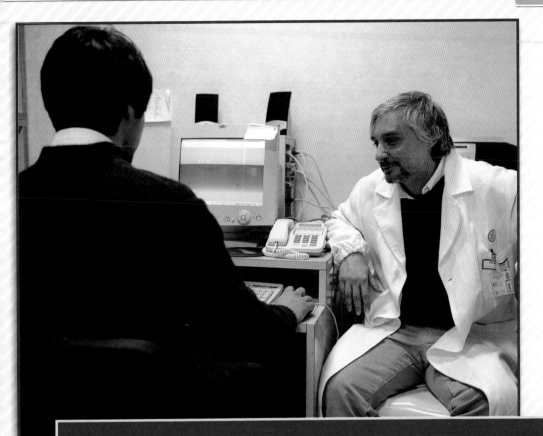

Clinical psychologists, psychiatrists, and social workers are all professionals who have expertise in helping people with depression. They work in many different settings, including clinics, hospitals, and private practice.

They will be able to provide many of the therapies described above. Many clinical social workers will focus on psychosocial issues faced by the patient, including those related to family, community, and identity issues.

The most important thing to consider when deciding which therapist to work with is if you like and trust the person. It may seem simplistic, but if you don't get along with the therapist, psychotherapy will probably be ineffective no matter what his or her qualifications are.

It is important to find a therapist with whom you feel comfortable. To find a therapist who is qualified in CBT, ask your personal doctor or consult the website of the National Association of Cognitive-Behavioral Therapists.

Therapy

Cognitive behavioral therapy (CBT) tends to be the psychotherapy form of choice for adolescents. A course of CBT treatment usually takes a relatively short amount of time—typically months and not years—and is goal-oriented. Instead of delving into your past or relationships with the people around you, the focus is on learning to see the connection between how you think and process things, how you feel, and how you act and relate to other people. You, your therapist, and sometimes your parents decide what specific issues you are facing, and you spend time working with your therapist on how to look at the problems realistically and how to resolve the problems in a healthy and effective way.

Your therapist is there to listen to you and is rooting for you to get better. For therapy to work, you must understand the goals and feel committed to them. During the first session, the therapist talks to you about your medical history, your family, and how you are feeling. A common course of treatment involves one forty-five-minute session a week in an office where you talk with the therapist about the problems you are facing and discuss your thoughts and feelings. Your therapist will help you identify any distorted thinking. You'll discuss how to correct this and map out healthier ways to resolve the issues in your life. You may be assigned weekly homework to practice skills you learned during your session. You may start to feel better after a few weeks of therapy, but it will take more time to get the full benefits of the treatment. Generally speaking, CBT takes somewhere between three and four months, though for teens suffering from severe depression it might take a bit longer.

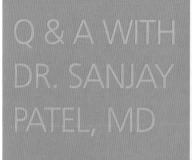

Q & A WITH DR. SANJAY PATEL, MD

What is your educational/ training background? Where do you work?
I am a child and adult psychiatrist, and I see patients in my private practice. I am also on the faculty at the New York University School of Medicine. I did my medical school and residency training at Mount Sinai School of Medicine in New York and then did a fellowship in child and adolescent psychiatry at New York University.

What do you find most rewarding about your job?
I am fortunate that I can help people improve their lives and become happier and more successful. Observing this change, which I see every day, is extremely rewarding.

Why did you decide to work with adolescents? What age groups do you work with?
When I was in elementary school, I already knew that I wanted to work with children when I was older. Today I see people of all ages, from young children to older adults.

How do adolescents suffering from depression usually first get referred to you?
Patients find me in all different ways: through their pediatrician, through schools, or through word of mouth, which is how most patients find me.

What things should a teenager (and his or her parents) think about when searching for the right therapist? What questions should they ask?
You have to feel comfortable with your therapist. Without that, it's

hard to start getting better. A therapist should be a good listener, respectful, and someone whom the entire family feels they can trust. If the therapist is considering medications, it's useful to ask about how the therapist will decide what the best route is, and what he or she will try to do with therapy before recommending medications. For instance, it might be important for some families to ask if the therapist is open to trying only therapy initially. Having a partnership with the therapist and the family is important for the success of the treatment.

What are some of the most common therapies you recommend to teenagers suffering from depression?
I believe teenagers generally should get cognitive behavioral therapy, which looks at the relationship between your thoughts, feelings, and behaviors. Families can be involved with therapy, but you don't have to do separate family therapy. Often it can be part of the teenager's individual therapy. At times, kids will need medication, and the safest choice is a class of antidepressants called SSRIs. The most common SSRIs prescribed are Prozac, Zoloft, and Lexapro.

On average, with therapy and/or medication, when do teenage patients start seeing some improvement (even if it is small at the start)?
Improvement should begin in the first few weeks. Even at the end of the first session, I want patients to feel more hopeful. Full recovery can take longer but usually we aim for significant improvement in the first weeks or months.

Do you have any words of wisdom that you would like to impart to teenagers who have been feeling down for a while and believe they might be suffering from depression?

(continued on the next page)

(continued from the previous page)

In teenagers, depression is typically a little different than with adults. When a teenager has a good experience, he or she might be happy temporarily and then go back to being depressed. That is normal for adolescent depression. Teenagers should understand that depression is a sickness and that they should stay hopeful because there are ways to get better and feel healthy and happy again.

Considering Antidepressants

For some teens suffering from depression, psychotherapy is enough. For others, it is not. Depression that is severe or has a strong hereditary/biological basis may need to be treated with medication. For many people, a combination of therapy and medication achieves the best results. Antidepressants are not magic pills that cure depression instantly, but they can make a significant difference. People who have been treated for depression often say that medication helped "take the edge off" so that they were more receptive to talk therapy. It is as if the medicine tones down the depression symptoms enough so that the person feels more open and motivated to work on therapy.

SSRIs and More

There are many classes of medications that are available to treat depression. These different types of drugs change the concentration of different neurotransmitters in the synapses, to improve the communication between neurons and to alleviate symptoms of depression. It is still unclear exactly how this mechanism works to improve the symptoms of depression.

For some teens suffering from depression, psychotherapy is enough. For others, therapy and medication together works best. Only a psychiatrist (or your physician) can prescribe medication.

SSRIs are a relatively new class of drugs that have the least troublesome side effects. Fluoxetine (Prozac), paroxetine (Paxil), sertraline (Zoloft), citalopram (Celexa), and escitalopram (Lexapro) are all SSRIs. This is the class of drugs that are deemed safest for adolescents.

Serotonin and norepinephrine reuptake inhibitors (SNRIs) and norepinephrine and dopamine reuptake inhibitors (NDRIs) are other classes of drugs that are sometimes prescribed to adolescents. There are other drugs that can also effectively treat depression, but they tend to cause more side effects.

The Downside of Antidepressants

A combination of drugs may be necessary for optimal results. However, only a medical doctor or a psychiatrist can tell you which combinations and which regimens are safe. Mixing drugs can be dangerous, and when taking prescription medications you must carefully follow your doctor's instructions.

It is important to note that medications for bipolar disorder are usually not the same as the ones that treat major depression. In fact, antidepressants can trigger manic episodes in those with bipolar disorder. This is why getting an accurate diagnosis from a mental health professional is key.

Antidepressants should only be prescribed by a medical doctor. She will have access to the most updated scientific research to make sure that if you do take medication that you take the best and safest one for you.

Another important thing to consider when taking antidepressants is that these drugs come with a black box warning (an official Food and Drug Association warning) that states that using antidepressants may cause an increase in suicidal thoughts or tendencies in young adults between the ages of eighteen and twenty-four, especially during the first few months of treatment. While a small risk of this exists, many experts say that the possible benefits of the antidepressants greatly outweigh the risks of untreated severe depression, which also puts young adults at a higher risk for suicide. Teenagers taking antidepressants should be monitored carefully by their psychiatrists or doctors during the first three months of treatment. Parents should be educated on how to spot warning signs that may signal trouble.

Just as with starting an antidepressant, changing these medications must be done under the careful supervision of a medical professional. Under no circumstances should a teen stop using an antidepressant or adjust the dosage on his or her own without consulting the medical provider. Doing so can cause serious physical and emotional withdrawal symptoms. It may even cause a relapse of the depression. Sometimes patients want to stop taking a medication because they do not feel improvement right away. It is important to remember that you need to give medicines a chance to work. For example, although some patients might start feeling better after a couple of weeks taking SSRIs, for many people it can take six to eight weeks to feel the medication's full effects. If the medical provider and patient decide that it is time to stop a particular medication, the plan will usually involve tapering down the dosage gradually instead of stopping cold turkey.

Antidepressants usually come in pill form and are taken once a day. You should follow the doctor's instructions carefully.

Antidepressants sometimes cause side effects. The most common ones are nausea, weight gain, drowsiness, insomnia, dry mouth, dizziness, agitation, irritability, and anxiety. These side effects usually subside after a few weeks. Still, you should report any side effects or reactions to your doctor. Remember, if one antidepressant does not work for you, your doctor will help you find one that does.

Some forms of depression are treatment resistant, or difficult to treat with the most common therapies. Fortunately, alternative therapies, like electroconvulsive therapy (ECT) or deep brain stimulation of specific areas of the brain, seem to be effective for some patients.

Empowering Yourself with Information

For most people with clinical depression, getting professional medical help is the cornerstone of recovery. Many teens find learning about the illness to be empowering and motivational. It also helps them be part of the decision-making process.

The amazing thing about the Internet is that it makes finding all types of information so easy. Research, statistics, and journal articles are literally at our fingertips. But with all of the websites out there that discuss depressive disorders, make sure you are getting information from trusted sources. Knowledge is power, but that is only true when the knowledge is accurate and backed by science and experience.

Ask yourself these questions when reading a web resource:

- Who wrote this article? Is it written by a medical doctor or mental health professional?

Learning more about depression is empowering and will help you make better choices. Researching reputable websites or reading a book by an expert are great ways to make sure you are getting accurate information.

- Has it been edited and reviewed, and is it relatively up to date?
- Who is the target audience for this article? Is the information relevant to you?
- Is the website affiliated with a respected organization, an educational institution, or a reputable company?

In additional to educational websites, there are also great nonprofit organizations that are focused on getting people help and providing information to the public. Several of these organizations are listed at the back of this resource.

CHAPTER 4

WHAT CAN I DO TO HELP MYSELF?

By now you know that getting help for depression is crucial. But we should talk more about one key piece of the recovery puzzle: you. Working on other aspects of your life in conjunction with treatment will give you the best chance to fight depression in the long term.

If your symptoms of depression are severe, you may need to be in treatment for a while before you have the motivation and energy to follow these suggestions. But if you feel like you can, pick one thing off this list that you think might be easiest to work on. You may be surprised that one small positive change can set off a cascade of bigger changes that you never imagined were possible.

Most experts believe that working out is a wonderful way to boost your mood. Additionally, exercise comes with many other health benefits. A great way to stay motivated is to recruit a work-out buddy.

Exercise

Work out. This may seem unappealing to some people not used to physical activity, but studies have shown that even small amounts of moderate exercise provide great benefits for body and mind. Experts believe that working out boosts your mood, improves your blood sugar regulation, helps you sleep better, increases your energy levels, and decreases the risk for count-less other health problems. The goal is to move more and to do something you like so you will stay motivated. Taking a walk around your neighborhood, finding a beginner's yoga class, or playing a casual ball game with a few friends are just some ways you can fit exercise into your busy schedule.

Eat and Sleep Smarter

Eating and sleeping well are also critical to your physical and mental well-being. You probably know from personal experience that not sleeping enough can make you grouchy and unable to concentrate. It can also contribute to symptoms of depression. Scientists have observed via MRI imaging that, when shown stressful images, sleep-deprived people have increased activity in the same areas of the brain that clinically depressed people do. Scientists believe that lack of sleep may inhibit the growth of new brain cells, which is also a risk for mood disorders. Teens should aim to get nine hours of sleep every night and to sleep and wake up at regular hours. A regular sleep schedule will help the quality of your sleep, and you will wake feeling more refreshed. Other benefits of good sleep are weight regulation, improved memory, and increased energy.

Just like sleep, what we eat impacts our minds and bodies. The brain needs a variety of nutrients to support all of its important functions. For example, omega-3 fatty acid, a nutrient found in fish and in certain vegetable oils, helps in the regulation of serotonin. Studies have shown that a deficiency in omega-3 can lead to symptoms of depression. The best bet is to eat a wide variety of fresh foods. Eating a balanced diet will help you get many of the essential nutrients. Avoid foods with a lot of sugar or caffeine, as too much can cause fluctuations in your mood and lead to symptoms of depression as well.

Eating well is also crucial. For example, too much sugar or caffeine can cause unhealthy mood fluctuations. Eating fresh foods and sticking to a low-sugar diet is also good for your skin, energy levels, and weight control.

Just Say No

Some teens suffering from depression turn to alcohol or drugs to self-medicate. While these substances may temporarily make you feel better, they can leave you feeling even more depressed once the effects wear off. Dangerously, the use of alcohol and some illegal substances can quickly lead to addiction. This is one of the reasons why many teens suffer from both depression and addiction. Substance abuse can be particularly devastating for teenagers because alcohol and drugs can have damaging effects on a teen's developing brain and body. It is easy to see how addiction and depression often become part of a vicious cycle. If you think you have a problem with drugs or alcohol, you need to talk to a trusted adult—like your parents, guidance counselor, or doctor—right away.

The Power of Human Connection

Studies have found that having a good support system and forming healthy attachments make teens more resilient. Think about which relationships are most important to you and help you feel good about yourself. Then think of ways that you can deepen those connections. Have dinner with your family on a regular basis, ask your best friend to sign up for a weekly art class with you, or try calling a favorite relative weekly to catch up.

Spending more time with family is a great way to feel more connected. How you decide to spend that time together will depend on the interests and hobbies of the various members of your family.

One way to connect with peers is to join an online support group or discussion board that is geared toward teenagers. It's important, though, to make sure that the group is part of a reputable and established organization and that you don't post any personal contact information online. A great place to start is on the National Alliance of Mental Illness website.

Connecting with a higher power and a faith community is another great way for teens to stay hopeful and feel supported. Reading about different religions at the library, attending religious services with a family member, or praying are just some ways that you can delve into spirituality.

Helping others is a wonderful way to feel more connected to your community. Volunteering to read to the elderly at a nursing home, tutoring kids in a subject you are good at, or helping clean up the neighborhood park are all ways you can volunteer, help others, and boost your sense of self-worth. Helping your friends and family in small ways will also make you feel more connected, add meaning to everyday life, and make other people smile.

Musical Therapy

Several studies have shown that music can help with symptoms of depression. Singing, playing, and composing music are all ways that people can express deep emotions. For people who may not be as musically inclined, listening to the radio or your favorite playlist has been shown to be beneficial as well.

Have an Open Mind

Being open-minded is another way to help oneself. If you are diagnosed with depression that is more difficult to

Music is a great way to feel better. A Penn State Study with college students found that no matter what music someone listened to, whether it was pop, rock, classical, or country, the listener's mood improved!

treat, your doctor might suggest another treatment in addition to medication or talk therapy. Additional treatments include ECT, deep brain stimulation, and biofeedback therapy (in which you learn the connection between your thoughts and feelings and your physical state and then acquire techniques to gain better control over your involuntary stress responses). Some doctors recommend alternative therapies like acupuncture, meditation, breathing exercises, massage therapy, or vitamin supplements. You might be surprised by what helps you. Alternative therapies should be recommended and monitored by a medical professional and should be considered supplemental to more conventional treatments.

PERSONAL EXPERIENCE: JESS G.
(CURRENT AGE: 30)

When Jess was in fifth grade, she started having severe stomachaches called abdominal migraines. At the same time, she started experiencing anhedonia, which meant she had a difficult time enjoying even her favorite activities. She started to miss school frequently; in fact, one year she was absent so many days that the principal wanted to hold her back a grade. Fortunately, she was still doing well in her classes and with help from her mother, she was not held back.

One day, after a chance conversation with a friend, her mom realized Jess might be suffering from depression. Her parents, who were very supportive of her, took her to a doctor who diagnosed her with major depression. At this time Jess was already taking antidepressants that were helping with the abdominal migraines. These happened to be the same type of medication that can treat the symptoms of major depression. Both conditions are believed to be partly due to low levels of serotonin in the brain, and some scientific studies have shown that the two disorders are in fact linked.

Jess struggled on and off with depression throughout her teenage years. She was prescribed medications like the antidepressant Prozac but wasn't fully comfortable with them for fear of feeling less like herself. As a result, she was inconsistent about taking the medication. This made the medicines much less effective than they could have been. She also started seeing a therapist for talk therapy but found it difficult to open up to her during their sessions. Additionally, she tried biofeedback and cognitive behavior therapy, which she found more useful because they gave her practical and concrete tools to work with.

After college, Jess started taking her antidepressants more regularly and realized that taking them each day did make them more effective and significantly improved her mood. She found that the medications did not change her personality, as she had feared when she was younger, but helped her become a better version of herself. As she matured she saw more clearly how her depression affected the people around her, and this motivated her to stay on her treatment. For Jess, of the types of treatments she attempted, the antidepressants had the most profound effect on her depression. Still, Jess wants teens to know that it often takes a lot of time and hard work to figure out what works best for each individual; but it is worth the effort because you can get better when you find the right combination of treatments and therapies.

Jess is now a family physician living in Seattle with her partner. In her work, she uses her own experiences to help others who are struggling with health issues. Like everyone else who struggles with a chronic issue, she has her ups and downs. Although she knows she will likely continue to fight depression throughout her life, she now knows that taking her medications regularly helps keep it under control. This allows her to feel better, enables her to have the capacity to nourish her relationships, and gives her the freedom to do the work she enjoys.

Change Your Perspective

"These experiences of darkness make the light more beautiful, that the pain of being acutely depressed allows you to experience an unbelievable happiness in every day when you aren't depressed and a sense that each of those days is a gift. So that's the real message of hope, is that you can get better. And when you do get better, not that you'll look back on it with great longing, but you may look back on it and think, 'I learned a lot by going through that. And I'm a better person because I did it.'"

—*Author Andrew Solomon, in the PBS documentary "Depression: Out of the Shadows"*

Don't underestimate the importance of having a healthy perspective. The idea is that you need to convince yourself that you want to get better, you can get better, and you will get better. To get in this frame of mind, sometimes it helps to make a list of all the positive things in your life that you are thankful for. This list will motivate you to get treatment so that you can again enjoy them. Struggling with depression is hard, and you should be patient with yourself. Don't beat yourself up if you have a bad day. But also, be patient with the people around you.

The key element of having a healthy perspective is staying hopeful. Remind yourself that there are many effective treatments today. Be encouraged that every day scientists are working hard to find even better ways to help those suffering from depression. Recently scientists have used MRI imaging to find that depressed people who show certain changes in part of the brain, called the anterior insula, respond better to medication. People who show

Try to keep a positive perspective. With help, you can get better. Be patient with yourself. Take time to celebrate small achievements on your way to feeling stronger and getting better.

decreased activity in that same area respond best to talk therapy. Findings like this will inevitably lead to more individualized treatments. There is great hope that in the future people suffering from depression can get treatments that alleviate their symptoms more quickly and completely. Know that though depression is indeed a difficult challenge, your struggles to overcome it can make you a more understanding and stronger person.

Glossary

ADDICTION An unhealthy dependence on something, such as alcohol or drugs.

ANTIDEPRESSANT A medicine that helps regulate mood by making sure the brain maintains healthy levels of neurotransmitters.

BIOLOGICAL Having to with living organisms or the parts of a living organism.

BIPOLAR DISORDER An illness that causes a person to suffer alternating periods of abnormally up and down moods.

CEREBELLUM A part of the brain that coordinates movement.

CEREBRUM The largest part of the brain, it regulates emotions, personality, learning, memory, and many other important functions.

CLINICAL PSYCHOLOGIST A professional who completed many years of graduate training (usually a PhD or PsyD) and uses various types of psychotherapy to treat patients suffering from mental health issues.

COGNITIVE BEHAVIORAL THERAPY (CBT) A time-limited treatment that helps patients change the way they think and learn practical skills to solve problems.

ELECTROCONVULSIVE THERAPY (ECT) A treatment in which electric currents are passed through the brain, causing a brief seizure.

GENES Inherited codes that serve as instructions to make proteins that our bodies need to function properly.

HIPPOCAMPUS An important part of the cerebrum that controls the formation of memories.

MAGNETIC RESONANCE IMAGING (MRI) A technique that allows doctors to look at the structure and activity of different areas of patients' brains.

NEURON A cell that uses electrical signals and special chemicals to relay messages between each other.

PERSISTENT DEPRESSIVE DISORDER A long-term depression with milder symptoms that lasts for two years or more.

POSTPARTUM DEPRESSION A kind of depression that some women experience after giving birth.

PREDISPOSITION A state of being more likely to act or feel a certain way or having a tendency to suffer from a certain condition.

PSYCHIATRIST A medical professional who specializes in treating mental health issues with medication and therapy.

PSYCHODYNAMIC THERAPY A type of talk therapy that focuses on helping patients understand why they are acting a certain way by examining and trying to resolve conflicts and issues from childhood.

PSYCHOTHERAPY A general term used to describe talk therapy that mental health professionals use to treat certain disorders.

SYNAPSE The tiny gap between two neurons or between a neuron and another cell.

For More Information

Anxiety and Depression Association of America
8701 Georgia Avenue, Suite 412
Silver Spring, MD 20910
(240) 485-1001
Website: http://www.adaa.org
ADAA educates patients and their families about depression, anxiety, OCD, and other disorders. It has resources that help them find treatment, information, self-help materials, and support groups.

Canadian Mental Health Association, National
1110-151 Slater Street
Ottawa, ON K1P 5H3
Canada
(416) 484-7750
Website: http://www.cmha.ca
This organization provides information about a variety of mental health topics, including youth and depression. Its website allows you to find your local chapter of the CMHA and provides information on mental health public policy.

Child Mind Institute
445 Park Avenue
New York, NY 10022
(212) 308-3118
Website: http://www.childmind.org
The Child Mind Institute website provides information on mental issues that affect teens and children, including depression.

It also provides tools for families to better understand depression and includes resources for how to find a qualified therapist.

Depression and Bipolar Support Alliance (DBSA)
55 E. Jackson Boulevard, Suite 490
Chicago, IL 60604
(800) 826-3632
Website: http://www.dbsalliance.org/
DBSA is dedicated to supporting people who are living with depression and bipolar depression. The organization has more than 700 support groups across the United States and a majority of its leadership has been diagnosed with mood disorders.

Freedom From Fear
308 Seaview Avenue
Staten Island, NY 10305
(718) 351-1717, extension 20
Website: http://www.freedomfromfear.org
This mental health advocacy organization was established in 1984 to support people who suffer from anxiety and depression. The group's website features links to associations and institutes that study mental health issues, as well as journals that publish scientific research on such issues.

Mood Disorders Society of Canada (MDSC)
Suite 736, 304 Stone Road West, Unit 3
Guelph, ON N1G 4W4
Canada
(519) 824-5565

Website: http://www.mooddisorderscanada.ca/
Established in 2001, but with roots dating back to 1995, this
    organization was founded to raise awareness about mood
    orders and available treatments for these disorders. It advo-
    cates for stigma-free programs to serve Canadians with
    mood disorders and their families.

National Alliance on Mental Illness
3803 N. Fairfax Drive, Suite 100
Arlington, VA 22203
(703) 524-7600
Website: https://www.nami.org
This organization provides information on mental illnesses and
    helps patients, families, and specific groups of people find
    support. The group's website creates a space for people to
    share their own struggles with depression and to read about
    other people's experiences. Its helpline (800-950-6264)
    assists people who are suffering from mental health issues,
    or their families, get the information and help they need.

National Institute of Mental Health
6001 Executive Boulevard
Rockville, MD 20852
(866) 615-6464
Website: https://www.nimh.nih.gov
The National Institute of Mental Health website provides infor-
    mation, statistics, and research information on depression
    and other mental health issues. The NIMH is part of the
    National Institutes of Health, and it focuses on research and
    development of treatments to help people suffering from all
    kinds of mental health issues.

National Suicide Prevention Hotline
(800) 273-TALK (8255)
Website: http://www.youmatter.suicidepreventionlifeline.org
This is the website for the National Suicide Hotline. It includes
    information about suicide prevention, and the hotline is
    available both in the United States and Canada for anyone
    who is having suicidal thoughts or thoughts of hurting
    themselves.

Websites

Because of the changing nature of Internet links, Rosen Publishing has developed an online list of websites related to the subject of this book. This site is updated regularly. Please use this link to access the list:

http://www.rosenlinks.com/ESS/Dep

For Further Reading

Andraka, Jack, and Matthew Lysiak. *Breakthrough: How One Teen Innovator Is Changing the World*. New York, NY: HarperCollins, 2015.

Field, Jon Eben. *Depression and Other Mood Disorders (Understanding Mental Health)*. New York, NY: Crabtree Publishing, 2014.

Giddens, Sandra. *Frequently Asked Questions About Suicide (FAQ: Teen Life)*. New York, NY: Rosen Publishing, 2008.

Hemmen, Lucie. *Parenting a Teen Daughter: A Crash Course on Conflict, Communication and Connection with Your Teenage Daughter.* Oakland, CA: New Harbinger Publications, 2012.

Letrain, Jacqui. *I Would, but My DAMN MIND Won't Let Me (Words of Wisdom for Teens)*. Seattle, WA: CreateSpace Independent Publishing, 2015.

Murphy, James. *Coping with Teen Suicide*. New York, NY: Rosen Publishing, 1999.

Nelson, Gary. *A Relentless Hope: Surviving the Storm of Teen Depression.* Eugene, OR: Wipf and Stock Publishing, 2007.

Niven, Jennifer. *All the Bright Places*. New York, NY: Knopf, 2015.

O'Hanlon, Bill. *Out of the Blue: Six Non-Medication Ways to Relieve Depression (Norton Professional Books)*. New York, NY: W. W. Norton & Company, 2014.

Oren, Goldie Karpel. *Yoga (Fitness for the Mind and Body)*. New York, NY: Rosen Publishing, 2015.

Schab, Lisa M. *Beyond the Blues: A Workbook to Help Teens Overcome Depression (Instant Help Book for Teens)*. Oakland, CA: New Harbinger Publications, 2008.

Schab, Lisa M. *The Self-Esteem Workbook for Teens: Activities to Help You Build Confidence and Achieve Your Goals* (Instant Help Book for Teens). Oakland, CA: New Harbinger Publications, 2013.

Schwartz, Tina P., *Depression: The Ultimate Teen Guide* (It Happened to Me). Lanham, MD: Rowman & Littlefield Publishers, 2014.

Serani, Deborah. *Living with Depression: Why Biology and Biography Matter Along the Path to Hope and Healing.* Lanham, MD: Rowman & Littlefield Publishers, 2012.

Styron, William. *Darkness Visible: A Memoir of Madness.* New York, NY: Vintage, 1992.

Travis, Richard L. *Overcoming Depression in Teens and Pre-Teens: A Parent's Guide* (Dr. T's Living Well Series). Seattle, WA: CreateSpace Independent Publishing, 2012.

Bibliography

American Psychological Association. "Understanding Depression and Effective Treatments." July 2010. Retrieved May 20, 2015 (http://www.apa.org/topics/depress/recover. aspx).

Brendel, David. "What Is the Relationship Between Depression and Substance Abuse?" ABC News. February 27, 2008. Retrieved May 20, 2015 (http://abcnews.go.com/Health/ DepressionScreening/story?id=4355978).

Burns, Tom. *Psychiatry: A Very Short Introduction*. New York, NY: Oxford University Press, 2006.

Child Mind Institute. "Major Depressive Disorder." Retrieved May 20, 2015 (http://www.childmind.org/en/health/disorder-guide/major-depressive-disorder).

Cobain, Bev. *When Nothing Matters Anymore: A Survival Guide for Depressed Teens*. Minneapolis, MN: Free Spirit Publishing, 2007.

Gonzalez, Sherri McGinnis. "Brain Networks 'Hyper-Connected' in Young Adults Who Had Depression." UIC. August 27, 2014. Retrieved May 20, 2015 (http://news.uic.edu/ brain-networks-hyper-connected-in-young-adults-who-had-depression).

Harvard Medical School. "What Causes Depression?" June 9, 2009. Retrieved May 20, 2015 (http://www.health. harvard.edu/mind-and-mood/what-causes-depression).

Mayo Clinic. "Teen Depression." November 7, 2012. Retrieved
    May 20, 2015 (http://www.mayoclinic.org/
    diseasesconditions/teen-depression/basics/definition/
    con-20035222).

Mental Health America. "Depression in Teens." Retrieved May
    20, 2015 (http://www.mentalhealthamerica.net/
    conditions/depression-teens).

Murphy, Caroline. "12 Surprising Causes of Depression."
    Health.com. Retrieved May 20, 2015 (http://www.health.
    com/health/gallery/0,,20515167_5,00.html).

National Institutes of Mental Health. "Depression in Children
    and Adolescents." Retrieved May 20, 2015 (http://www.
    nimh.nih.gov/health/topics/depression/depression-in-chil-
    dren-and-adolescents.shtml).

Nationwide Children's Hospital. "Sleep in Adolescents (13–18
    Years)." Ohio State University. Retrieved May 20, 2015
    (http://www.nationwidechildrens.org/sleep-in-adolescents).

Schwarz, Alan. "More College Freshmen Report Having Felt
    Depressed." *New York Times*, February 5, 2015. Retrieved
    May 20, 2015 (http://www.nytimes.com/2015/02/05/us/
    more-college-freshmen-report-having-felt-depressed.html).

Solomon, Andrew. *The Noonday Demon: An Atlas of
    Depression*. New York, NY: Scribner: 2002.

TeensHealth. "Depression." Retrieved May 20, 2015 (http://
    kidshealth.org/teen/your_mind/mental_health/depression.
    html#).

WebMD. "Teen Depression." March 6, 2014. Retrieved May 20,
    2015 (http://www.webmd.com/depression/guide/
    teen-depression).

Index

S

T

About the Author

Y.S. Lin graduated from Brown University with a bachelor of science in neuroscience. After graduation, she moved to Manhattan and worked in the educational test prep and publishing industry. She is now a writer living in New York City with her family and has written a series of short children's books on famous scientists from the past.

Photo Credits

Cover © iStockphoto.com/mathiaswilson; p. 5 Knauer/Johnston/Photolibrary/Getty Images; p. 6 PamelaJoeMcFarlene/E+/Getty Images; p. 9 Christopher Furlong/Getty Images; p. 10 Universal Images Group/Getty Images; p. 12 Image Source/Photodisc/Getty Images; p. 13 Tay Rees/Stone/Getty Images; pp. 16-17 Science Source/Getty Images; pp. 21, 30 BSIP/Universal Images Group/Getty Images; p. 25 Jetta Productions/Digital Vision/Getty Images; p. 27 Imagesbybarbara/E+/Getty Images; p. 29 Andreas Solaro/AFP/Getty Images; p. 35 Jonathan Nourok/The Image Bank/Getty Images; p. 36 Jamie Grill/Getty Images; p. 39 Roberto Machado Noa/LightRocket/Getty Images; p. 41 Chris Baldwin/Image Source/Getty Images; p. 43 George Doyle/Stockbyte/Getty Images; pp. 44-45 Klaus Vedfelt/Iconica/Getty Images; pp. 46-47 Inti St Clair/Blend Images/Getty Images; p. 51 Hero Images/Getty Images; back cover and interior pages background pattern ONiONA/Shutterstock.com

Designer: Nicole Russo; Editor: Amelie von Zumbusch;
Photo Researcher: Nicole Baker